Endorsements

"Rachel Leah's blessed work is inspired by her understanding that soul and spirit are real, and that human consciousness is eternal, infinite, and immortal. She embodies wisdom and compassion, the hallmark of all great healers."
Larry Dossey, MD, author of
One Mind: How Our Individual Mind Is Part of a Greater Consciousness and Why It Matters

"Rachel's work reminds us that we are all sacred. She shows us how to reconnect to our soul. This book can help us die consciously and with the heart full. An important book for the expansion of consciousness."
Ondrea and Stephen Levine, authors of
The Healing I Took Birth For: Practicing the Art of Compassion As Told to Stephen Levine; and
Who Dies?: An Investigation of Conscious Living and Conscious Dying

"As a midwife of dying, Rachel Leah offers an expanded paradigm for people who are dying and heart-centered wisdom for their loving caretakers. She reminds us that love is the glue that connects dimensions and invites us to practice letting go of our attachments as we live life fully so that our final surrender is as natural as our out-breath.

"Part personal story about one woman's journey to embrace her soul-centered service and part practical advice, SAFNAH Death-Birth Threshold is a treasury of experiential insights and practical wisdom. I appreciate Rachel's clarity and groundedness as she puts words to dimensions that are almost ineffable."

Rosalie Deer Heart, author of
Healing Grief: A Mother's Story; and
Soul Befriending: High Beam Living and Loving

"I am so grateful to Rachel Leah for writing this unique and important story of how, since young childhood, she has acted as a sacred midwife to lost souls and to those who are dying. As you travel through these pages, may her stories inspire. May they transform your relationship to death, and to life."

Llyn Roberts, MA, author of
Shapeshifting into Higher Consciousness; and
The Good Remembering: A Message for our Times

"This book has helped me realize that I am not alone. I am not the only person struggling to feel open about my gift. This book will stay floating in the back of my mind for many years to come. For those days when I am in doubt about speaking to others about my soul purpose of assisting others, this book will be remembered. A life-changing read!"

Lauren Cox, Student

SAFNAH

Death-Birth Threshold:

*The Conscious Movement
from the Physical Body into the Life Beyond*

*Donna —
Happy journeys and
easy thresholds.
            Rachel*

Rachel Leah

SAFNAH
Death-Birth Threshold:

*The Conscious Movement
from the Physical Body into the Life Beyond*

Copyright © 2015 by Rachel Leah

All rights reserved. No part of this book may be used or reproduced by any means, graphic, electronic, or mechanical, including photocopying, recording, taping, or by any information storage retrieval system without the written permission of the publisher except in the case of brief quotations embodied in critical articles and reviews.

ISBN: 978-0-9965785-0-9
ISBN: 0-9965785-0-1
Library of Congress Control Number: 2015946356

The information, ideas, and suggestions in this book are not intended as a substitute for professional advice. Before following any suggestions contained in this book, consult your physician or mental health professional. Neither the author nor the publisher shall be liable or responsible for any loss or damage allegedly arising as a consequence of your use or application of any information or suggestions in this book.

Cover design: Audrey Jordan, Visions of Heaven
Back Cover Photo: Heidi Jordan

Sacred Life Publishers™
SacredLife.com
Printed in the United States of America

Dedication

To my parents Katherine and Samuel
who, with love, supported me
each in their own way.

To my children Sunshine and Jacob
who always believed in me and encouraged me.

To my grandchildren Oliver, Lilly, and Mackenzie
who are lights to this world,
forming the future.

Contents

Endorsements

Dedication v

Introduction *Now Is the Time* ix

Preface *My Understanding* ix

Chapter 1 *My Call to Service* 1

Chapter 2 *The Die Is Cast* 9

              Coincidence? 10

Chapter 3 *The Forgetting* 15

Chapter 4 *Choices* 23

Chapter 5 *Transformational Death* 27

              Claire's Story 29

              Sophie's Story 31

              Julie's Story 32

              Dan's Story 33

Chapter 6 *The Grand Surrender* 39

              Carol's Story 41

	The Grandmother's Story	41
Chapter 7	Hereafter	45
	An Unexpected Message from the Other Side	46
	Stan's Wishes from the Other Side	47
	A Joke on My Father	48
	Love Begets Love	48
	The Energy of Working Through Life's Challenges	49
	Sue's Story	52
Chapter 8	Time of Death	53
	Gloria's Story	55
Chapter 9	My Process	59
Honoring Life's Process		63
Acknowledgments		65
About the Author		69
Glossary		71

Introduction

Now Is the Time

Did you know that there are people here in the physical world who are able to assist your spirit in leaving your physical body at the time of death? These gentle guides can help you safely cross death's portal to join with those "on the other side" who will welcome you home. This threshold, between life and death, is called *SAFNAH*—the combination of two Hebraic roots. It is time to bring this in-between work to the public. This is the work I've been doing since childhood. We live in a time of fear and darkness as well as of greater spiritual light. As more and more people wake up to who they truly are–consciousness—we can reclaim our capacity to be aware as we transition from physical life on earth to our true spiritual home.

Welcome to my world-on-the-edge, this is my life's work that requires a presence that can navigate two awarenesses. I hope you will find this book supportive, encouraging, hopeful, and caring. My prayer for you is that when the time comes to transition from this life, you will be supported by what you discover in this book–that is, to embrace love over fear and depart this earthly experience with clarity and grace.

Preface

We all wonder how and when we are going to die. To some, death is scary and not the sacred time it can be.

Fear is not a natural state of consciousness, it is learned. Throughout this book I will remind you that we all are sacred, and that where we come from is the home base to which we will return.

I do not want you to be afraid of death, nor afraid to die. My purpose in writing this book is to support you and all people at the transitional point of death. The fact that I can assist in this transition has been something I have kept in the dark for too long. My experience has shown me that we do not have to be afraid to die.

My Understanding

When we are born, we are open to the wonders of life and unlimited potential. Then we have experiences of loss and pain, and are also conditioned to fear death and the loss of physical life. In becoming overly attached to the material aspects of the world, we can lose touch with the sacred and get caught up in fear. Ideally, we can grow through life's experiences and awaken our potential as a divine spark of consciousness. As we become more aware, we can express ourselves as free, creative souls.

In my world, there are greater losses than that of dying. There seems no greater loss than that of our soul connection; that deep awareness supports us in feeling fully alive with a sense of adventure and curiosity, despite being vulnerable, physically or emotionally challenged, and even knowing we will die. When we can let go of our fear, all the divine gifts we have come into this world with can flow and be shared and also help us grow on our earthly path. No matter who we are and no matter what we do while we are here, if we remain true to our gifts, leaving this physical reality can be experienced peacefully and gracefully. We can be awake and aware as we die.

We can decide to die consciously, just as we can decide to live consciously. Within every experience is a decision point: how will we handle the experience? Will we open and learn, even if it is a difficult experience? Or, will we avoid it as an enemy?

Life is a continuum–an unfolding process wherein hope dwells and an individual's reality can be manifested. Physical death is a reality, yet the idea that spirit dies at the time of physical death is illusion.

In the following pages I discuss and explore the following concepts and experiences:

> ➢ How I came to work with people in transition. The struggles I had in accepting my place in a society that did not speak my language–my philosophy about life and death. How the goal

of not having souls trapped here, as ghosts, became a journey into myself and service for others.

- How we forget where we come from before being born. Why, although we come to earth with under-standings, some of us forget while others choose to remember both their purpose and where they have come from.

- How the process of dying and ultimately the experience of death transform us. What the barriers are to transformation and how we might move beyond them to a conscious passage from this life.

- How we leave this physical form and what support is available, if needed, for a wakeful death. I call this section "The Grand Surrender," the conscious release from the physical form into the next expression of "life."

- How the hereafter is comprised of boundless love that transcends death and connects our earthly life experiences with what we experience after death.

- How and what tools can be utilized at the time of release from the physical, and how we can help others both in the physical and in spirit form.

➢ How some of us create and support a gentle passage and how some people can be a bridge to show the way out of physical existence and into the spiritual realm.

In this book you will find validation for experiences and understandings that lay outside our conditioned reality. For those of you who aren't sure about the continuum of life (yet are open to the possibility), and to those who believe there is nothing beyond the physical life, may I plant a seed of doubt.

Chapter 1

My Call to Service

A learning disability is a difficult experience, but not necessarily a curse in life. In school the message I inferred was that I was stupid because I wasn't learning the same way everyone else was. I was put into a "slow learning" class. I remember riding in the car one day, looking out of the window thinking, "If I don't smarten up, I will be born retarded next time." Where did a nine-year-old come up with a concept like that when there was no conversation about such things in my environment? I, as do many children, came in with understandings brought from previous lives. Not that I would be slow next time, but that there was a "last time," and there will be a "next time." What having a so-called learning disability did for me was allow me to find my learning elsewhere. I withdrew, hid, from the world around me and enjoyed the world within. I was often found gazing out of the window and was told to "do something"! I was doing something... traveling.

As a preteen, I would travel, in consciousness, outside my physical body into places of Light, where I learned about perspectives I hadn't consciously previously known. Then, coming back to this world, I would bring with me a Love so great that I often sensed no ground beneath my feet. I would close my letters to people with the phrase "Within the Love." I always capitalized the "L" in love because it seemed that Love, as it flows through the heart, is the greatest power–so filling and encompassing that all else is obliterated and true peace is experienced. The Divine Light, depicted in religious paintings, shows us the way. "Within the Light" is the greatest wisdom–the light exposes and reveals the truth within all experiences. Within the Love and the Light is limitless possibility and while possibility is limitless, as a child without any foundation on which to build, I felt directionless.

Then, one summer, I unexpectedly received the verification from my community on Martha's Vineyard Island that set me on my course.

My aunt had a house on a bluff overlooking Lagoon Pond on Martha's Vineyard. According to the guest book, my parents stayed there in September and I was born the following June. Perhaps being conceived on Martha's Vineyard set a pattern of new beginnings for me on that island. This has continued to be the case through the many decades of my life.

My family stayed all summer, every summer, within a community of "Summer Vineyarders" who swam, played, and picnicked together on the beach; we embraced each other's lives, and that is how the first validation of my experiences appeared.

Chapter 1 – My Call to Service

S. Ralph Harlow and his wife, Marion, who had built their summer home about the same time that my aunt had built hers, were just a few minutes walk away. Ralph Harlow had a doctorate in theology and was a prolific traveler and writer in support of humanitarian issues. One of Ralph's books is *Life After Death*. Two of Ralph and Marion's children, along with their spouses, built and shared a house on the lagoon. We all lived in close proximity. My friends were the grandchildren of Ralph and Marion. Every Sunday evening as my friends passed our house to go to the Sunday Night Sing at their grandparents, my parents, siblings, neighbors, and I would join them. I remember so clearly sitting in their living room, feeling how full it was with loving spirits. I came to learn that my friends, parents, and grandparents were Spiritualists who held séances to get in touch with those who had passed from this life and were experiencing life beyond the physical.

One particular incident changed my life.

Marion told her children that she had written a word on a piece of paper and placed it in an envelope in a bureau drawer. She said that, after she died, she would get in touch with her children and in her message would be a word she had written, thus proving beyond a doubt that there was life after death. Marion died in 1961. Within a year of her passing, her children received a letter from a medium in the Midwest. My understanding at the time was that the medium had researched the family to find where Marion's children lived. This memory is unclear. The medium stated she had received a message from the spirit of Marion Harlow and was told to send it along to her children. The message read, "You have never seen such Light as there is here." At that point her children opened the envelope and found the one word their mother had written: "Light." That story has always stayed with me as proof of the Truth I intuitively knew.

The next major turning point for me in planting my feet firmly on the ground of Spirit communication came when my family moved to Newton, Massachusetts.

My elementary and high school years were spent in Newton. My life seemed normal from all outward appearances–hanging out with friends, going to movies and dances, etc. Yet, internally I was at odds as my interests were starkly different than my friends. I became bored, depressed, and felt very alone. There was no one to tell my journeys to, no one who would understand where I was going, and what I was seeing was much more enjoyable than what I could get from a book. Parties did not hold my attention. As I moved through expected social interactions, I was screaming inside. In retrospect, this strange and uncomfortable time was an important turning point in my life.

In our Newton, Massachusetts home there was an active spirit in his astral body form. This spirit was someone who had died decades earlier, and was now opening and closing the creaky attic door to get my attention. Until my high school years, I slept with the light left on, thinking doing so would block out this spirit. I knew that this spirit was attempting to get my attention, which it did with all its noise. I could see his smoky form standing on the threshold of my room. Because I didn't know I had the ability to help him, I attempted to block

Chapter 1 – My Call to Service

him out and felt a bit frightened, though he never tried to hurt me.

Then, one evening when I must have been feeling brave or curious, perhaps both, I asked him why he was hanging around. He told me he was afraid to leave the earth field because he had impure thoughts while in his physical body. I found I was not only able to hear him telepathically but was able to respond to his fears. Through the love and compassion I felt for him, I explained there was no one judging him but himself and that it was safe for him to move along. At that time I did not realize I was going to be able to show him the way, but for then he seemed complete with our conversation.

While in high school, I became interested in astrology through readings on comparative religions and metaphysical teachings. During this time, I was told that there was an astrologer in Boston, Isabel Hickey. She taught meditation as well as astrology and spoke of angels and departed souls. Fondly known as Issy, she became my friend, teacher, and mentor. I attended her Friday night meditation classes and enjoyed going to Harmony Hill in Nottingham, New Hampshire on summer weekends, planting gardens, and learning and sharing with Issy. It was with Issy's guidance that I helped release this stuck soul, or ghost.

One evening, as I sat visiting with a couple of friends in the living room of our home, there were noises coming from upstairs. The three of us were the only ones home– that is, in the physical. I explained to my guests about the man in spirit form who lived up stairs. We agreed to see what we could do to assist the ghost's release.

I called Issy, who always made herself available. She give us the following guidance: 1) visualize the room filled with Light and surrounding us, 2) say a prayer, inviting those on the other side who knew and loved this stuck individual to come to his aid. We followed her directions.

Following Issy's directions three spirits then appeared as pillars of light. Their light shimmered like the light of the sun illuminating falling snow. Inside, I felt honored that the prayer had worked! I was in awe of the stillness that filled the room, the purity of silence and the power of love manifested. I intuitively spoke to the stuck spirit, even though speaking in my physical voice seemed ludicrous considering the circumstances; I gave him permission to leave, "within the Love" and, along with these three light beings, he did.

My friends and I all felt the shift of energy in the room as the four souls vacated my living room; a sense of stillness pervaded the space. Just as one feels after having had company for a time–when they leave, there is new space felt. During this experience I was so focused on the experience and what I might be called to do that my friends had vanished from my awareness. It wasn't until the spirits left that I noticed my friends again. We didn't even mention what had happened because we decided to go into the cellar to sneak a smoke and talk.

A few minutes later, there was a very loud noise as if lightning had struck the ground. The three of us looked at each other with fright and concern. We dashed upstairs not knowing what to expect but there was nothing–no

Chapter 1 – My Call to Service

smell, no tree through the roof, nor door smashed in. I decided to definitely tell Issy about this in the morning!

The next day Issy explained that the spirit was just saying thank you and good-bye in the only way he could by making the sound of jet breaking the sound barrier.

To assist a soul in moving into the light and into the love of spirit in order to reunite with loved ones who had already made this transition was a profound experience for all three of us. I felt liberated. Love and direction filled me. I knew then that I had a reason for my untypical interests.

It was during and after these experiences with the Spiritualists at Lagoon Pond and with this earthbound spirit that my friends and I had assisted that I thought, "This is not right. People need to be shown how to leave and be given permission to move on."

The sadness I felt for the tormented man stuck on this plane of existence and the love I felt coming from the attending spirits and through me, started me on my journey. My goal became to stand on "the other side" saying, "Come this way" to the departing souls. At my young age, I imagined that directing souls to the other side meant that I could hang out in my spirit body between the here and there, directing transiting souls like an elementary school street crossing guard. Little did I know what adventures I had set into motion.

Chapter 2

The Die Is Cast

It is thirty years ago now that I decided to work with the elderly to position myself to work at death's gateway. I found myself being unable to turn away from the ongoing information I was becoming so familiar with inside myself. I finally decided that I would find some scientific support for working with people even though that support would be more peripheral than specific to my vision of the purpose of my "gifts."

I first became a Certified Nursing Assistant. Then I received a certification with the American Red Cross in Advanced Emergency Care. Finally, I earned another certificate in Gerontology from the University of New Hampshire. At that point I set myself up in business as a respite caregiver. Going into homes, I assisted the families who were caring for their aging loved ones. While doing this work, my learning and inner teachings continued. I found myself in situations in which people benefitted not only from my practical assistance but also from my unique perspectives on death and dying.

Coincidence?

One day in 2001, a friend, Marie, asked me if I would like to meet a spiritual teacher just back from teaching in her community in Brazil. This teacher, Sophie, had moved into a nearby assisted living and nursing home to retire and to be near her sister, who was also in the home. I told my friend that I didn't want to see Sophie. I had no need of a spiritual teacher because I had my inner guidance.

Several weeks later, as I walked up to another friend, Jane, at the local Farmers Market, Marie suddenly showed up, too. Marie said to Jane, "My friend Sophie is dying. I must leave and go to her." So Marie left the market. This coincidence was too startling for me to ignore. I then returned home where I held an internal vigil that day, keeping my attention on this woman, Sophie, whom I had never met. I remained open for any use I could be to Spirit.

The following week when I saw Marie, I asked her how her friend Sophie was doing since I had heard that she had not yet passed into the next realm. I knew that Marie, who had a family, was going in at every mealtime to feed her, so I offered to relieve Marie and take a meal shift. Marie agreed and that is how I finally met Sophie.

Sophie and I began spending time together. One day she shared that she didn't understand why it was taking her so long to die. I suggested that she had gotten very used to giving to others and that her heart and love had become used to outflowing to others. But now it was time

Chapter 2 – The Die Is Cast

for her to go within so she could prepare for her spirit to be drawn out of her body.

Over time, I had discovered that the doorway to wisdom and knowing opens inwardly. We each must withdraw to our center to do this. Often, my spiritual students who learn that they can travel out of body also assume that they can just pop out of their own body when it's time to pass over to the other side. This has not been my experience.

So, one evening, Sophie was close to death but was not quite ready. It was very late, and I had said my good nights. I had told Sophie that I would see her in the morning. She reached her hand out to me and said, "Don't go, you are the oxygen."

Although I had no idea what she meant, I stayed. Holding Sophie's hand, I suddenly found myself out of my body while I remained connected to her. I saw a tunnel and at the other end of the tunnel were people bathed in light. In my inner vision I could also see Sophie looking up at me. Then the words came: "Come this way." She didn't leave or pass within that moment; however, there was a gift that she was giving me–she let me know that she was consciously present within the experience with me. When I came back to the physical perspective, she said, "I failed." She meant that while we were both out of body, she assumed that she would and should pass then. I told her, "No, this is not something you can fail." There is a mystery about when we leave that is part of the process. We can prepare to leave, but the timing is not ours to assume.

The next day when I came to see her again, the medical curtain had been pulled around Sophie's bed. She was unresponsive. As I psychically viewed her body, it was evident that she was still connected at her heart center and had a bit of congested energy around her left shoulder. Not having my tool, a gourd rattle, with me that I often use to break up coagulated energy, I snapped my fingers within the area and swept the air around Sophie's shoulder with my hand. After clearing the energy at her shoulder, I concentrated on her heart, asking my spirit guides inwardly, "What do you want me to do?" The answer came: Instead of bringing aspects of consciousness back into the physical as you typically do with Soul Retrievals, you are to release the conscious Earth expression of Sophie's Soul. Leaning over her heart I breathed in, feeling her essence come into my own heart with my breath. Then, I exhaled her essence out and up, visualizing the Light. Feeling complete, I said my goodbyes and returned home.

At around 6 a.m. the next day, I called the nurses station and was told that Sophie had departed earlier that morning. I immediately went to the nursing home to make sure Sophie had made a complete transition. As I sat with her body, Sophie appeared to me in the form of the blue Brazilian Morpho butterfly that she so loved. The butterfly then transformed into Sophie as her Spirit herself. "Thank you," she said. Then she disappeared.

Thank you, Sophie, for showing me that the work I have been shown and called to since I was a young child is real and valuable, not an illusion.

Chapter 2 – The Die Is Cast

For me, this proof, if you will, has given me a grounding beyond ego or imagining something. The completion of the process and the visual and auditory information is not something I can simply bring to myself or dream up. It is always an unexpected gift that reveals the truth of what I am doing. There is no way to count on what or when I will find that external mirror saying yes, this is truth.

Chapter 3

The Forgetting

If children were permitted to experience life from the center of their being, as they do when they enter the world, the ebb and flow of events would not have as much weight as they do when we attach to our experiences; attachments can become values with little substance. The reactions of others can also create conditioned responses to experiences. For example, children look to adults to know how to react when they fall, get hurt, and when they achieve something.

Imagine if, when there is loss, it is viewed as an opportunity of growth, an opening to another life experience! Just because one is sad does not mean that the experience is not an opportunity. In detaching from past and future we can view life as a string of experiences like pearls creating a beautiful necklace. In staying centered within the moment, what we have learned in the past is here now, while the future can be created each moment because we are present.

When we set a goal every step taken, within the moment, is toward that end, because the mind has not set limitations, when the goal is set within our heart. We start making decisions sometimes unaware of why a decision is made until we look at the place where we have arrived, closer to our goal.

When I made the decision to help others across these two worlds, I had no idea how that goal would be reached. I went down the path unfolding in front of me. A friend suggested I look into Hospice. Hospice was close to my goal, but not it. That is when setting myself up in my own business was realized, which led to certifications. For me living within the moment and paying attention to what is going on around me is similar to being in a state of meditation; we are centered and connected to our high consciousness and, therefore, available for guidance, beyond the mind, to reach those goals. It is important to remember where we came from that we have Soul awareness and gentle guidance which comes from that connected state of consciousness.

The following is a touching story given to us by a child about the return of a Soul, which seems so perfect. I wish we all would listen to the wisdom of our child self before the world comes into consciousness and the veil of forgetting shrouds our vision.

It was the year 2003. I bought a picture for my granddaughter's birth at a health expo. The picture depicted a sweet little boy, about the age of five, standing next to a crib and looking up at his much younger sister, who, in turn, was looking down at him. The picture had such a feeling of comfort and love that I wanted the print for my new granddaughter's room. Because she had a sweet older brother, I thought it a perfect gift. The people from whom I bought the print informed me that a real life story had inspired the painting: The five-year-old boy in the picture had repeatedly begged his parents to be allowed to go into his sister's room, alone. The parents had concerns about the boy and his intentions toward this potential rival. They relented after many requests although they had great trepidation. Allowing their young son into the room alone, the parents kept a close ear to the door. They heard the older brother's request of his baby sister. "Please," he said, "Quickly, tell me about God before I forget."

Plunging into this life we forget. Our journey to identify with this new life begins to take over our consciousness at birth. Our previous existence and knowing move into the distant past as our new experiences take form: our attention shifts to the material world that is currently in front of us.

When we take on physical form, life becomes more about survival and less about who we really are. From the beginning we must learn how to communicate in order to have our needs met because we are so unable to care for ourselves. As babies, we coo and giggle, receiving pleasant acknowledgment from the people around us. When we are hungry or uncomfortable, we come to see that our cooing and giggling does not always produce the response required to get what we need; however, we discover that crying does. We begin to learn about cause and effect, which become tools for survival. The forgetting deepens.

Some survival tools can become encumbrances. Mentally going into an itemized detailed list of reasons for doing something or not can become a means of habitual protection, born from fear of making a mistake or being misunderstood. In generating mental tools, we may hold ourselves back in the process of other possible actions by closing the door of consciousness. It's important to remain open and flexible to new possibilities, options.

Dependency can, unconsciously, take us further from the center of our being. As adolescence approaches, independence becomes the goal. The adolescent, still dependent on an adult, will fight tooth and nail to get his own way. Existence becomes a tearing in two directions, while any prayer for balance and peace remains elusive. It is important to grow through dependency to be able to release the hold on an attachment. In order for us to be at peace, we must learn to shift from battle and, at some point, to surrender and accept change, accept a new way of existing more fully aware of who we truly are becoming.

We not only outgrow parental dependence, but we are also challenged to choose self-acceptance as an independent expression of life in order for balance between the battle to survive and peaceful surrender to occur. When we accept our choices through our experiences we recognize who we are not, and who we are—our reflection appears.

If we don't find self-acceptance, the reflection is not a true one. For example, when a person finds emotional or spiritual security through someone else, the self can be forgotten. Angry people may get into relationships that end up supporting their anger. Responses become habitual; they may drift along in life unaware they are

Chapter 3 – The Forgetting

supporting each other's attachment to a past negative experience. How can there be can growth when neither owns their anger? Without independence, there cannot be self-acceptance because we then rely on another's mind set and opinion. Self-acceptance based on living in someone else's reflection of fear and anger can leave as quickly as it came. Soul will cry out for recognition; it's up to the individual to hear the cry. That cry is felt as pain.

A child, from the beginning, needs to be able to hear his own voice within the chaos of the many voices. When I mentioned to a friend that their adolescent children were so open and gracious and engaging with others, her response was, "We tried not to mess them up." Eventually, people must wake up to the fact that they have identified their life with the tools of their survival: denial, projection of personal issues on to others, attachments to people, places, and things, and anger as rejection.

The fight for Soul survival becomes a personal reality. People can forget their true identity, as Soul, meaning as an independent, conscious, co-creator of life. Soul has no attachments to physical and emotional survival tools and is, therefore, not afraid of losing any one of them. When there is no fear of loss, there is no fear of change and no fear of death.

Life continually gives all of us challenges that need solving. An independent, self-secure person will see those challenges as simply that–challenges. She or he will take it upon herself or himself to explore how to solve an issue. A person who has not yet created self-supporting tools for survival, or who has not recognized her or his own worth and abilities, can feel threatened and overwhelmed, victimized, angry, and even turn to various means of escape. When we are not up to life's challenges the concept of death is yet another threat to avoid.

The irony is that as individuals begin to acknowledge death, the door to life opens wide. Every time a person releases the attachment to a physical and/or emotional experience or surrenders to the unknown, a new expression of self arises. For example, releasing a relationship that is dysfunctional because it is based in fear is a paradigm shift: I am this, not that.

The creative power within an identity may show itself. For example, a doctor may realize the Healer is within self. The doctor as mechanic may then become the intuitive channel. Or the adult reconnects with the infant self who was connected to the divine. We each can become a creative adventurer. We can return to our core–Self.

Before we take the plunge to this Earth, we were all we had learned, a collection of awarenesses and perceptions without the encumbrances of our physical survival tool bag. Once here, over time we devise formulas and mental strategies that give us a sense of security. We trust these perceptions, histories, and hold onto outlived modes of operation even as our habits become encumbrances.

The unconscious shift from the free flowing adventure of life to a linear survival mode based on non-acceptance comes from the world of musts and shoulds.

Chapter 3 – The Forgetting

We become what the world accepts and reflects. We lose the trust and wisdom that when we are perfectly ourselves we will not only survive but we will thrive.

Children at play are simply having experiences. Play is the discovery of action and reaction: if you do this, you create that, and when you do something else, a new something is created. Possibilities are endless and the adventure has begun.

As we experience a renewed sense of self, we discover that it is possible to create new experiences, adventures into the unknown, and to become an exploration of self. We can also go a different path: the child becomes a young adult, finding and building survival tools, identifying self with those tools, and forgetting who he is as a creative individual at play manifesting his existence in the sandbox of life. This forgetting of where we come from may become a barrier to an easy transition from the physical.

What can you create? Freedom is born from growing from the battle to survive to yearning for the survival of self. So, too, acknowledging the loss or death of something opens us to the creation of something else. Surrender to possibilities accepts the notion of the more, limitlessness contained in form–a paradox. Death, the letting go of attachments and the identity of self via old survival tools, allows life, the shifting into acceptance of the possibilities of a new awareness of self.

Chapter 4

Choices

A young man I knew, John, was the first middle school student to manage a high school baseball team, and, as it happened, that year the team won the series for the very first time. Later, in high school, John wanted not to manage anymore, but to play and be on the team. Now, this young man had a major challenge to achieving that goal, he was asthmatic. John knew he had to increase his lung capacity and endurance if he was going to make the team.

Every day John would run on a dusty, hilly roadway. He steadily increased his speed and endurance, never missing a practice. The tryouts were in the final stages and on the last day, it rained. So, the coach decided to have the challenge to making the team in the school gymnasium. The competitors were to show how they would slide into a base; they had their sneakers on. When it was John's turn, he caught the edge of his sneaker on the wooden floor and broke his ankle. When the list was posted of who made the cut, John's name was on the list; he had reached the goal of being on the team, but not the one of playing. John spent that season with his foot in a cast simply watching from the sidelines on the bench.

John then had a choice of how he would process this huge disappointment. He could go down a dark path of anger and bitterness, or do what he did. John said, "I wonder what I'm supposed to learn from this?" I can speculate on what he learned; how strong and resilient he could be. If John had chosen to be and stay angry, he would have been stuck in the place of forgetting who he truly was. He would not have moved forward in life. Instead, he chose wisely. John grew into a responsible, caring adult who embraces challenges as opportunities. John recognizes he has freedom of choice and the ability to attain goals.

As the mind stores information, we work off that information in daily life. Whether we are secure in our potential as free creative beings, or fearful of every step we take shows in the choices and decisions we make. Even physical pain, which we all avoid as best we can, has a method of being released, taught in child birthing classes: breathe in, release out, and the body relaxes.

We can train ourselves to notice how our body constricts when our thoughts and feelings are fear-filled.

Fear and attachment go hand in hand and pain is the result. How we choose to respond to life's experiences can either support, or suppress, our deeper expression. We all know what it feels like to be stuck in a relationship, job, or partnership that is not healthy for us.

The daily news is full of stories that depict the challenges and choices individuals make. Some of them are inspiring while others leave us scratching our heads.

Chapter 4 - Choices

One person finds the strength within, the self-support, and builds a foundation for the next experience, while another may lash out at a cruel and unjust world, placing blame, and not accepting personal responsibility.

In John's case, he could have placed blame on the coach, perhaps rightfully so, but to what end? What would have been accomplished that would have benefited John? The choice John made defined who he was as consciousness. So, too, at the time of death, consciousness can help determine how we face that next step.

Consciousness is not segmented; life is a continuum. Our experiences, thoughts, and aware-nesses are tied together like a holographic string of DNA. It may appear that someone is "growing up" when in fact, that person is waking up. In looking back on life we may see that where we came from and where we are now has been a single path toward remembering our true self. That is–who we truly are at the center of our heart.

The openness that a baby comes into the world with can be experienced at the point of death. Embracing life within death moves the sacred spark of the divine from this state of life to the next, home.

Chapter 5

Transformational Death

A bud becomes a flower, a caterpillar becomes a butterfly; when the physical body is no longer needed by the soul the body dies and the consciousness, Soul, is released.

When one thing dies, space expands and the potential is open for a new expression of life, a transformation. Death is never a single experience. Death is experienced on many levels by all: emotionally in releasing heart-centered attachments and mentally in releasing conceptual attachments. Physical death is only one aspect of life. Creation expands when we let go and expand. For example, we have ideas that shape our reality, as in, "I will never accomplish my dreams because I'm not as bright as others." We cannot transform when we are attached to a misconstrued belief system.

When a person sets a goal to be the best carpenter, teacher, or artist, he or she needs to release the fear of being able to achieve that goal. With focused intent we can plunge forward and transform ourselves as we create and express our goals.

As we release outlived concepts, we are drawn toward other goals and new experiences. The transformation is complete when we recognize this self without doubt and fear. It's often then that our goals become secondary because we understand that the process of transforming is primary. This wisdom renews our confidence and brings our essence to the surface. We are transformed.

There are so many small deaths within a lifetime, losses that seem huge at the time. Things we have identified as being our own reflection: property, jobs, or relationships of all kinds taken from us, given away. This is all a rehearsal for the Grand Surrender.

When the time comes for us to say, "Good-bye, thank you for being here. I love you" by the person leaving, those who remain must also release us and the past–and embrace the possibilities before us.

Those who have the opportunity to watch their own aging process have time to co-create their transformation from their past to their new beginning. They have the time to surrender and reconnect to the possibilities of the adventures from childhood. As elders our responsibilities are done; it's time to draw on experiences and see what remains true during all these years to discover what our Truth, our core, is.

To grieve is to acknowledge and honor our own process; to mourn is to hold tightly to the attachment. To grieve the loss of a dream is to feel the life of it within our heart. To mourn the dream is to live in its past reflection, holding to an image that has since been transformed.

Chapter 5 - Transformational Death

To grieve the loss of a parent, a child, spouse, or dear friend requires going through the process of letting go and honoring that heart-felt relationship. To mourn that relationship usually has attachment to it . . . an incompletion, the I should have said or done something. For example, one kind of incompletion is that of the dream lost for writers who have a book within them and who did not carry through with the writing.

In the end, if the heart is not acknowledged, not expressed, it becomes a heavy burden to carry. To grieve the end of a marriage if it just didn't work out is complete, whereas to mourn the end of a relationship while thinking that if only you had done more doesn't allow the heart to feel complete.

The following stories describe how some people processed the act of transforming from this expression of life to the next.

The ghost in the Newton house could not release from life on earth until he recognized that his was a story based on outdated information. This entity had lived with fearful visions of doom and gloom during his physical life and then carried that belief with him even though his body no longer held him. It wasn't until he was taught a new paradigm that he was able to release his attachment to this life and freely move on.

Claire's Story

Claire was in her nineties and had been facing health issues, but had not yet outwardly acknowledged that she might be preparing to leave her body. During a visit, we had time to sit and chat. I asked her about her religion, knowing she was a Baha'i, and what that faith meant to her. As I watched her search for the words, she also searched for the connection. She was remembering and experiencing being in that space of devotion within herself. It was a meditation for her as she voiced her convictions to me. I suggested she might enjoy a visit from a friend who was also a Baha'i. From what I later heard, Claire renewed contact with a group of Bahai's that met regularly. I do not know if she had one-on-one conversations, but what seemed important was for her to continue a connection she rediscovered within herself.

The importance of the time we sat together was Claire's ability to shift into that centered meditative state–which revealed the knowing within her faith. Claire had been so caught up in the battle to survive her life had been consumed by it. She owned her battle; in other words, she was identifying with her pain–it was an attachment, as in my pain, my cancer, my battle, my existence.

Being reminded of her faith shifted Claire's awareness from the struggle to survive to her spiritual self. She began participating in the process of transforming old patterns by simply shifting her attention. As of this writing, Claire is still with us, doing her inner work. One day there will be nothing more she desires or can do, and she will surrender this physical world. Her identity with this world will be transformed into a new identity, a new learning about who she is.

Chapter 5 - Transformational Death

Sophie's Story

Remember Sophie and my first experience as an intercessory? Discussing with Sophie how she had lived her life as a teacher helped her understand what I shared with her about the energetic flow of consciousness at the time of transition from life.

Thought contains energy–think of it as a picture the mind sets up when emotion is fed into it. When this is followed by action, there is an energetic flow of consciousness. That is the way we set and accomplish our goals.

When you set a goal you are also telling the Universe to support your intentions. The support that arrives can seem magical. Simply put, where we place our attention is where we consciously exist.

If the attention shifts from the outward flow to the inner core, there is relaxation, acceptance, and peace. That transformation allows the release from the physical form, including when that form can no longer support the life force. Our consciousness is then drawn out to a place that does support life. Death is an illusion. Life continues, transformed into another state of experience.

Once Sophie realized that even her life of service could be an attachment to the physical, she began her journey to release all ties to this world.

Sophie's body grew weak until finally she was unable to sit up in her chair and had no interest in food. While holding her hand one evening, I was taken out of my form and could see light and people behind me. I could see Sophie in my inner view looking up at me as I said, "Come this way." She had thought that this meant that she had failed to die, but what she had done was give me the gift of knowing I could do what I, since childhood, had wanted to do–show people the way home.

Sophie left her form within twenty-four hours of this experience.

Julie's Story

Sometimes a person stays because he or she does not know there is anything else–doesn't know that transformation is even a choice.

Julie had been diagnosed with dementia and her son perceived that she needed guidance. Her son asked me if I could help his mother. What I always say is, "I don't know, but I will try."

The aids brought Julie to her room and helped her sit in a chair. She looked at her son who was sitting to her left and then she looked at me sitting in front of her. I greeted her by introducing myself. Julie then did what her son reported she never did; she reached for my hand. As I held her hand, I was able to view her at play as a young adult, jumping hurdles with her teammates. The joy and freedom she was experiencing was palpable. As we sat together, I was able to give her back that experience. I was able to feel that energy of consciousness, known as Julie, jumping hurdles. Without speaking the words in my physical voice, in silence, intuitively I explained that she could have that feeling again, that this experience now of existing was not all there is. As her son and I left the room, I turned to say good-bye and, again Julie did what she no longer seemed to be able to do, she said "Thank you."

Julie left this Earth plane within two weeks of my visit with her.

Dan's Story

I was asked by an oncologist to visit a fellow who wanted to learn how to do a shamanic journey before he died; but that wasn't what the visit was really all about. Dan was holding on to his work with young people and had to release that attachment before he could find peace and release his form. Dan had been a counselor of youths with dependency issues and was very devoted to his work. The love that flowed through him was a blessing to experience. In this instance, Dan had surrendered everything except the job he had poured his heart into. As I sat with him, holding his hand, he was able to feel within my words the love and knowing of what was going to be there for him on the other side. He began to understand not only with his mind, but with his heart that he could continue his work on the other side.

When a person dies, the emotional attachments they have get carried along with them. If a person has an addiction when he dies, there are teachings and understandings that continue because consciousness does not die–it grows in awareness and is transformed. Once Dan realized his learning and growing in the physical and skills he developed within his beloved work could continue, there was peace.

It was not long before Dan surrendered his attachment of his work here and transformed it to the work he was yet to do.

§

Transformation cannot happen without surrender. And surrender cannot happen without the will to transition from one situation to another. When a person feels stuck within a job, a living situation, or a relationship, there must be the willingness to surrender being in that circumstance in order to have change happen.

It is true that *will* can be a double-edged sword. We can tear our selves down through willfulness to get an end result. This is where that co-creator partnership comes into play.

A dear friend and mentor, Gladys Widdiss, a Wampanoag elder on Martha's Vineyard, taught me a very valuable lesson. Despite the fact that some situations need to be given attention, that something needs to be done, if Gladys was not in the mood, she would not take action. She knew that if she was not in the mood, she was not within the natural flow of the unfolding of her life in relationship with the rest of the universe, and that there was something else for her to be accomplishing at that time.

It is important to be aware of how we are feeling as we strive toward goals. If there are obstacles that have no resolve we feel frustration. Then we constrict the body and the flow of our consciousness. These are signs that a

Chapter 5 - Transformational Death

given path may not be appropriate at that time. However, a person does not say, "I am not going to work or attend school because I am not in the mood." That doesn't benefit the whole in terms of necessary income and long-term goals of education.

Using both the left side and right side of our brain we can determine the practical timing for getting a goal accomplished. The left side will help us with the linear (what, where and when), while the right side provides the inspiration, the intuitive process. With an unconflicted mind, we are capable of benefiting the whole of humanity and ourselves through an open heart.

Accepting all that we cannot change, we will find it easier to surrender to the creative flow and reach the goal. This kind of acceptance opens the door to creativity, the ability to perceive, and to intuit solutions to achieve the goal in a peaceful environment of a transformed self.

Any relationship we yearn for must have appreciation and acceptance, whether with another person or with our self. Once both have been established, the relationship can be transformed as the concepts of must have's and must be's are surrendered and released, the creative process can begin within a new experience.

The question is how do we get to that point of surrender in order to transform a relationship or experience? Resignation comes when we have had enough. This is the time just before rebirth, transformation, and can involve pain at an emotional or physical level. Personally, when I realized it was time to live my calling to *SAFNAH*, all of the old programming of who I had been had to be released.

The time had come to expand my perception of myself to a broader view. My body reflected the shift with pain just as toxins in our body being released give us aches and pains. When we hear Soul's call to be released from an experience because the experience denies Soul's full expression, we usually can expect great turmoil to accompany our changing. We wrestle with releasing the familiar, which is no longer needed for our greatest good and, therefore, not the greatest good for all. Staying in a relationship because the change is terrifying denies growth. Our consciousness is trapped in an expression that no longer reflects who we truly are. Transformation in the midst of loss is an unknown. We struggle with simultaneous secondary losses in the midst of this unknown outcome—loss of self, loss of love, and even loss of the will to survive.

To accept suffering as a part of our life turns our back on the options of love and a life of grace. Surrender through relinquishing the hold on must be's transforms us and readies us for the next phase of life, thus demonstrating the power of love to draw us back to our true selves, Soul.

Willful intent is an ego-based mental prison that cuts others out of our possible community of understanding and growth. If any relationship is one-sided, it becomes a dictatorship, not embracing the expression of love, and it will eventually fail through isolation. When we are able to recognize that as Soul we are whole, we will not be threatened by relinquishing perceived need for authority. We become part of the universal community and cannot become isolated.

Chapter 5 - Transformational Death

Transformation can only happen through an interchange of thoughts, ideas, and through cooperation. Grace, through the surrender of our egos' *will*, creates life experiences in which we will have no loss of self.

Love does not die: it is the cohesive force, which brings experiences to us that reflect love. We must recognize our own ability to love to be able to accept love. We are always drawn to love as much as we allow it to exist. Love is not experienced by the mind, but through the heart. The more consciously we allow Soul and its divinity of love, the greater the cohesive force of that love and the greater and more meaningful our experience.

Life, that force that runs through the physical body, plants, and animals, our innate intelligence that we attempt to understand through science, is a creative continuum. This kind of intelligence does not turn on and off like a faucet–it continually flows, even at the time of physical death.

When the physical body dies, this innate intelligence simply withdraws into another space and continues life elsewhere.

As each life moment follows the last, one day into the next, each experience opens to growth, so too our conscious expression of life and of love.

We have losses and deaths and are reborn multiple times emotionally, mentally, and spiritually day after day. We lose friendships, jobs, ideas, and so on. This pattern does not change when our physical form no longer functions. Creation is powered by love. Life supports love. We strive to survive because of love. We transmute experiences because of our will to survive, to survive death within the love. In other words, where there is no longer love, the Soul cries out to be recognized and expressed. This is where marriages dissolve, children leave home, and people crumble into depression. Where there is no love, there cannot be a full expression of life.

In order to relinquish our hold on this physical life and allow the transformation from this view of the physical to a different view with fewer limitations, we surrender to a new creation. Surrender can be a conscious choice or something we finally give in to.

Chapter 6

The Grand Surrender

I call death the Grand Surrender because we do not push out of our body nor are we cut from our body. The Grim Reaper does not exist; there is no entity coming along to sever the life force from our form. Looking at the description of being cut from something, there would be a piece remaining. At the point of departure, we are drawn out from and release the body.

There is help for going through this process. Here in the physical world there are conduits: people who are called to guide others through the dying process, to be bridges and show the way. This is my calling. As a *SAFNAH,* I place myself at the threshold of birth and death, of death and rebirth, for others.

Sometimes at death's doorway I perceive there is an intermediary that I refer to as a "Death Angel." I may see this as a shadow. When I see that shadow pass through a room I know that the time of the person's transition from this world is close.

When I see the black energy move through the room, I am aware, that it is time to offer my services as a conduit and remain centered within myself and within the Love; my attention is focused in conscious prayer.

I have been asked why this entity appears as a dark shadow form when we are traditionally taught that angels are white. I had to ask this entity, "Why are you so black?" The answer was immediate as a wave of the purest love and compassion enveloped me: This intermediary can absorb and channel the vibratory rate of the departing consciousness in order for it to be transported from one place to another.

Light is expansive and creative while black is passive and absorbing. The dark angel allows us to withdraw from one experience and move into the Light of the next. Compassion is Love, and Love is the cohesive force. In safety, we glide from one embrace to another.

We prepare for death from the moment we arrive in this world. Everyday we compare our life experiences with whether something is in accordance with our center. Where we see ourselves, in our actions and reactions, in what feels comfortable and what does not, these are the values we create over time. As we determine our values, we create our identity, a sense of self. Then we may have peace within. Our struggle is over because we are able to be comfortable with who we are as an identity.

In coming into a physical form, we bring wisdom with us that we use to grow and expand–in other words, we come to earth with building blocks, a matrix creating a picture of the self. When this life comes to a close, Death asks us to release all of our collected experiences of this life, retaining only those that are the core lessons. The values extracted from life lessons become part of that matrix of wisdom. The spiritual growth we attain is carried forward through consciousness.

Carol's Story

Carol lay in bed, unable to hold herself up, unable to eat, no longer in control of any bodily functions. Still able to speak, she asked me, "What can I do?" Carol was a woman who was always forthright in actions and words, never one to beat around the bush. I knew my response had to be the same.

I answered, "There is nothing more you can do." Within three hours, she had passed from her physical form. Carol died the way she had lived, direct and to the point. She saw what she needed to do and did it, with courage and purpose. She surrendered to her next experience.

The Grandmother's Story

I received a call from a young woman who was with her grandmother in a nursing home. In fact, there were several family members visiting this grandmother and they had been there for three weeks. All of the visiting family was exhausted, in anticipating that this elder was about to die. They did not want her be alone.

The nurse in charge suggested they call me. The granddaughter and I talked for quite some time over the phone about what worries her grandmother might be having. Grandmother did have a worry that her grandson was unable to visit. Once the granddaughter and I recognized what was keeping the elder here, the granddaughter became more clear about what she could do to help her grandmother release from this life.

The granddaughter told her grandmother the boy could not visit and then she lay down beside her and sang. At home in my chair, I traveled inwardly to the grandmother and spoke to her about releasing her concerns and asked her to follow me by keeping her focus on me as we moved toward the great space within the Light.

When the struggle at death is released, time is irrelevant. When a Soul moves out of the physical form there is no concept of time and space–that belongs to this world. There is only the now.

A few days later, I received a call from a friend who worked at the nursing home telling me the grandmother had left her form within a couple of hours after the phone call made by the granddaughter.

The granddaughter had done a beautifully loving job of soothing her grandmother with words and then lying down next to her and gently singing. What a magnificent gift that young woman gave to her beloved grandmother! Because the elder and I had done our journey together, she knew where she was going and did not look back. There is an important point here about that part of the transition from here to the other side.

At the time of death, as the Spirit leaves the form, there is a portal of time that creates a clear and easy passage. As time moves on, it's like an ice flow moving over a body of water. An opportunity passes. That is why it is so important that whoever is present at the time of

Chapter 6 – The Grand Surrender

death is supportive and not clinging to the person. This is not to say that the departing Spirit is trapped here forever, but that it will take some time and, sometimes, more assistance to go beyond this plane of life.

Many of us have worked hard in the struggles of identity to come into an expanded self-realized state. Some may be aware of this journey and others may not. In the final hour, no matter who we are, everyone departs. What determines the experience of departure is how far we have come in the process of surrendering the past and embracing the adventure of a future. Those who have released attachments move on with grace, integrating back from where they came, more evolved. Those who maintain the struggles with attachments to this physical world, though their body can no longer hold their life form, may, as consciousness, remain. These entities can be seen and felt as ghosts. At times, the departure is not The Grand Surrender.

Fear begets fear. In the dying process, we must release limiting concepts of life and death, vessels that hold us in bondage: physically, emotionally, mentally, and spiritually. Setting ourselves free while still here in our physical form allows us to pass from this life consciously–with grace and within the Love. In our lifetimes, we have many opportunities to practice the art of surrender, releasing mental concepts and allowing the creative, expansive experience of embracing the flow of life within and around ourselves. Love embraces all–here and after.

Chapter 7

Hereafter

Death and time are illusions. Death appears as an end, as though something is here and then it's gone. Time seems to move on like water through fingers. When a loved one passes from our environment, the grief ebbs and flows. One is fine and then, like fog rolling in, comes the pain of loss . . . loss of love, and, yet, it is that very love that is present within the pain.

In diving deeply into the emotional pain, it is possible for us to find, at the other end of that dark tunnel, the light of love. Here on Earth, pain cannot exist without the love that caused the pain–the other side of the same coin.

Loss of a loved one through death is exceedingly painful because of the physical lost time together, the emotional joys and shared sorrows, and the spiritual connection of eye-to-eye and heart recognition that are no longer tangible.

When we acknowledge our loss, our love for the person who has left our lives seems as if it is under a magnifying glass, so huge, and in fact, it is. Time exists for us daily and is one reality, however, time no longer exists when basking in that love that we shared with our loved one. For instance, do we feel the passage of time within a loving embrace? No. Within that moment there is no time and no space, only the present, now. When there is the release of the embrace, the love we had shared when holding the person we care for never dies and is forever locked within our conscious memory. The sun rises and sets–a marking of time. Our lives go on, we change, but we carry the constant–that moment when time stood still and nothing existed except for our shared love.

Love as a cohesive force cannot be severed–it draws to itself reflections of mutual support. As love grows, consciousness changes and expands awareness. The conscious self is able to embrace more of life. This reflection of self may change, explaining the coming together and separating of friends and things. As we experience living here, there are difficult times, learning times, and growing times. Death is one of those times. Embracing the love we have for someone departed draws us closer to the departed because there are fewer encumbrances on the other side. There is more freedom of expression to simply . . . love.

An Unexpected Message from the Other Side

A friend and I were visiting one day and she mentioned her deceased mother-in-law. My friend was hoping she was all right and doing well. Within that moment, I saw the face and head of a woman by my friend's shoulder. The vision was smiling happily pointing to her wavy hair. I mentioned what I saw to my friend who, at first, could not relate to the women pointing to the hair. I double-checked what I was seeing to make sure it was accurate and the woman continued to point to her hair. Then my friend remembered–her mother-in-law loved having her hair done!

What a simple and yet profoundly touching moment for that mother-in-law to reach out from the other side to relieve my friend's concern about her.

Often times, the deceased loved one wants to, needs to, communicate that she is all right and sometimes pass along information that is needed by those remaining. Impressions of loved ones can ebb and flow, seeming to be mere memories, but when those memories feel palpable, perhaps a departed one is visiting.

Stan's Wishes from the Other Side

Stan, when he passed, was in his mid-fifties, leaving a family and siblings. His life had been expressed in many creative areas and he had been exploring having his art publicized.

Shortly after his passing, his wife and sisters came to me in hopes of connecting with him. Sitting together, his message came through loud and clear. His creative expressions were for his creative expression and less important for the general public. It was not necessary for his family to spend time and energy completing something they thought he wanted. In this instance, Stan's message concerned the well being of his family. He wanted to relieve their concerns about him and his life's work.

Stan also wanted to support his wife's intuition that she could feel him holding her at night while she went through her grieving process. His statement clarified for her that it was not her imagination, but that he was, indeed, with her at these times.

Expressions of love are magnified when they are shared. Though the loss of her husband left this woman feeling alone in the darkness at night, and sad by day, knowing that Stan could still be with her eased his wife's passage back to living her life. Out of that darkness a beautiful light of awareness within the love continues to evolve for this loving wife.

A Joke on My Father

My dad once told me that, in Judaism, there is no talk of what happens after death, because one cannot know. At his funeral, I saw two balls of light that came from the back of the room. They hovered over his casket and then were gone. Now my father knows—life continues. Death is simply a shift in consciousness.

Love Begets Love, Begets Love, Begets Love

A person shares the Love as it flows through him or her to another, that person is uplifted and shares with still another, and so it goes, tying us one to another. These are our teachers, the people who are the inspirations to be at peace and carry on, not only survive the pains of life, but thrive through the lessons and hardships that come with life.

To find that still point within the love where nothing else exists, to be able to release the experience of pain and find within its center the core of love–that is how we grow within these experiences as diverse as humanity itself.

The Energy of Working Through Life's Challenges

Each and every one of us is consciousness, which some call Soul, an expression of wisdoms collected as lessons are learned throughout our many lifetimes. That unit of awareness has a vibrational rate. I liken it to a note on a piano or a tuning fork. That vibration, which is felt as energy here in the physical body, has gone through layers of filters before being expressed in the physical form. These filters tone down the vibration of pure spirit so that we will be in balance for the lessons that will be learned in our physical lifetime.

This energy passes through the filter of the higher mind, intuition, through the mental realm of thought, and then to the heart and emotions. We can feel that vibration when we are around others–and be either comfortable or uncomfortable with that person's presence.

What makes each of us different from one another are the different lessons we learn while we are here in body form. Our lessons are housed within different aspects of consciousness that our soul has passed through. The services offered and performed, or not, are within each lesson at each level of awareness.

I personally had the experience of viewing a past life where I was treated horribly. I was both abused and demeaned. That viewing gave me two understandings: one, why I have never been interested in going to that country, and the other came when I asked why I'd had that experience in that lifetime.

The answer came swiftly, "You learned compassion, didn't you?"

When a person comes into this life with a strict rigid way of thinking, which limits spirit, that person may have the experience of eventually being born into a family that does not allow creativity and self-expression. The child is crushed and may need to struggle to gain the ability to express a broader view. Perhaps that person had inflicted judgments on another in the past. Then again, that struggle may be there simply to learn how to be strong, to move toward greater self-expression.

Understanding this can help us accept the differences in people who surround us. We may find that there are some people we simply don't want to be around because their vibratory consciousness is not comfortable for us. We may never know why.

As we learn these lessons, we incorporate them into our consciousness and, over time, a new mode of self-expression is produced. As well, our personal vibration is refined and, therefore, changed.

When we hold onto anger and pain, but then learn how to release and forgive, we experience changed consciousness.

Some of us are born into poverty, some into wealth, some into a violent world, and others into a more peaceful life. What we each do is in accordance with what we came into this world with as our core values–meaning what we are to experience and learn in order to come into a fuller expression of our self as Soul.

Because life is a continuum, our lessons are carried with us as we grow in understanding. As a child grows into adulthood he or she learns and makes decisions as to how to express what we know in this life. So, too, the entering soul makes decisions on what lessons need to be learned in order to grow into full soul consciousness.

Compassion is an important life lesson. Let's say an individual was a tyrant in a past life, and this time is born to experience what had been done to others in the life before in order to see that his or her actions were not the way of divine love.

Pain and suffering are constricting and limiting while compassion is expansive and peaceful. That soul who had the experience of being a tyrant now has the opportunity to learn what she or he would rather express. That conscious expression of soul becomes more evolved. The person's vibration is elevated as attachments that do not serve higher values are released. Through this journey, changes in consciousness can create a clear unobstructed channel of and for love.

When our vibration changes, our life changes because we cannot live outside our own vibrational rate. Some call this the spiritual law of karma, meaning that over lifetimes, our physical body, mental patterns, and emotional attachments are either released as lessons learned or are carried into the next world of self-expression.

Sue's Story

Sue, who had been widowed while I helped care for her, once asked if I had seen her husband, Louis. Because I hadn't, and she had asked, I went into meditation to look for him and see what he was up to. I saw him at a distance. Not wanting to disturb him because he was talking with someone, I stayed back and observed. It was obvious to me that Louis was being shown aspects of his life here on Earth for the purpose of showing him what he had learned. Louis, in seeing his lessons learned, could then consciously utilize these learnings that were now his gifts and values.

All the gifts one comes into this life with are from lessons learned and are now services to be performed for others. What happens after death is the same thing that happens here, only easier and more sweetly because we are among kindred souls–family, friends, and teachers. The afterlife schooling doesn't have the edges it does on Earth and the experiences are processed more efficiently, without attachment. When we are in the middle of an experience, it can be difficult to see its value. When that experience is completed we can have a new perspective from a different vantage point.

Chapter 8

Time of Death

As death draws near, love can feel amplified as if it is condensed within the moment. All memories can be viewed through the eyes and emotions of love and there can be visions of loved ones. The veil between the physical world and the finer worlds of existence begin to lift. We may witness the departing person reach out for someone who may be invisible to us.

As the body starts to shut down, linear consciousness begins to release its grip on time and becomes more centered within the moment. The conscious mind becomes more finite as the infinite spirit of consciousness becomes more present. Awareness moves away from the physical surroundings.

This is the time for us who are in the presence of this "grand surrender" to be detached and yet to remain within the love, to say in silence or to speak of gentle visions or to sing peaceful songs of gratitude.

I once witnessed both a distraction and a support in the same evening of a person's passing. One of the caregivers was sitting at the foot of the bed as we gathered around our friend. I noticed this caregiver tapping the dying person's foot. Was she tapping out her own concerns or nervousness or attempting to be reassuring? Who knows? What she was doing was drawing his attention to his feet. When the caregiver got up to go to the bathroom, I took her seat so that when she returned her place was no longer available.

Later, when I left, saying my good-byes, the dying man's grandson was sitting by his side speaking softly about peaceful sunsets and visions of beauty. Within two hours I received the call of the man's passing. His was a peaceful and supported death within the love.

It is important that we not call the departing person back. This may seem like an obvious statement but when we are attached to our loved ones we can become very distraught. This was brought home to me when I was hired through an agency to care for a man and to support his family.

The man had been moved in his hospital bed into a sitting room adjacent to the living room. It was a beautiful room overlooking the ocean that he had so enjoyed. As I was doing my duties straightening up the living room, I saw a vibratory image of the man sitting in a chair, as his body lay quietly in bed. I knew this man was getting ready to permanently leave his physical body.

At that time I made a conscious decision not to say anything to his daughter who was in the kitchen. I made that decision for a couple of reasons: (1) because it would probably sound crazy to her that I had seen him in a

Chapter 8 – Time of Death

vision, and (2) I sensed that she would become very emotional and attempt to call her father back.

A few moments later I went into his room to check and the man was gone. I suggested to the daughter that she might want to go in the room to check on him. When she saw that her father was gone, she threw herself across his body and began to wail. It was then that I knew my instinct to be silent was best for this man who was ready to leave this world.

Gloria's Story

Here is a final story to demonstrate the power of letting go, of acceptance, and the power of love.

At the time of writing this book, my friend, Ben, passed over. I was in contact with his wife, Gloria, and because the experience was so fresh I asked permission to write about their experience. Gloria gave her permission. I then inwardly asked Ben if he would relate his experience. The following is their story.

My long time dear friend, Gloria, was married to her husband Ben for forty years. Both in their sixties, they each had active and creative lives. One day, Gloria went off to ride her horse leaving Ben at his computer hard at work. On her return, Ben was still at his computer. Gloria thought he had fallen asleep while working, but he did not respond. Ben had slipped away while she was gone.

This kind of sudden death is usually not only disruptive to the one left behind, but can also be disorienting to the consciousness that has departed.

Their entire lives changed in dimensions without notice. No part of life remained the same for either one of them. Ben was in the physical world thinking very linearly about life here, and then, his perception changed–his conscious mind saw more around him, he could move more easily, he became acutely aware that his scope of perceptions had expanded. He felt lighter and at the same time confused.

Fortunately, Ben was accustomed to moving into creative and inspired spaces. He recognized the potential of this new experience. As he had recognized love while here, with Gloria and with animals and nature, that capacity to love drew Ben into the higher realms where he was greeted by similar Souls. After Ben got his bearings as to what had happened, he was able to come back, not as a ghost, but as a loving partner, to help support, guide, and teach his dear Gloria.

Gloria was in a whirlwind of shock and the business of dealing with the physical-ness of death. It was through the support of dear friends and family that she carried on through the first steps of her process of coping and managing life. Gloria was always a spiritual person who could find joy and who, also, was able to allow herself to feel pain. What she did with this traumatic experience was inspiring to watch and an honor to hear.

Gloria started to take care of herself so that she could survive. She found a drumming/journey circle led by a compassionate and educated woman. Because of her experiences with the drumming and journey circles I had held when we lived closer to each other, she knew this

Chapter 8 – Time of Death

would be healing for her and help her in her way to finding answers and release stress.

Gloria then found a Rolfer to get the bodywork done that she knew she needed to release tensions in different areas of her body.

And then there was her deceased husband Ben who would show himself to her in very endearing ways to let her know she was not without him. Gloria works as a nurse in the neonatal ICU on the night shift. In their life together, sometimes when she would come home from work, Ben would have supper ready for her that often included her favorite, brownies. One evening, after Ben had passed, after her shift, Gloria came home to the smell of brownies. This very physical sign warmed her heart. That is not all that Ben did and continues to do for her.

Ben is on the other side of this life and is seeing and learning, and understanding principles of life both here and beyond. He is teaching Gloria how to experience everything in this life without having those experiences destroy her spirit; she is learning that she is not those experiences happening to her. Through ongoing communication with her deceased husband, Gloria is experiencing firsthand that death is truly an illusion and that life here is an experience our Souls are having. Because she is open to doing so, Gloria is experiencing that there is life within death and that, indeed, love is truly the cohesive force.

Ben's most recent communication was, "We will get through this."

Chapter 9

My Process

People often ask me how I know what to do for people at the time of death and how it all happens. I am including this information to help detail my process.

When initially in the presence of a person on the threshold of transiting the physical, I bring myself to the center of my being and still my mind. When I do this, my inner senses become more attuned to the surroundings of that person and where she or he is in his process. I intuitively scan the body to see whether the person may be energetically held back by a congested area in the energetic field, as I did in the case of Sophie when I removed congestion at her shoulder and the attachment at her heart.

I cannot tell exactly when a person is going to die, that is not my job. My job is to guide the person across to the other side. This is done in one of three ways depending on whether the person is consciously connecting to the other side or has gone deeply within the self.

If the person's eyes are open, I will look into her or his eyes and speak what words come to me. If I see a spirit form in the room, I silently acknowledge its presence and inwardly support it in connecting with the individual who is preparing to leave. I do not interfere with the connection between the two souls because the one already in spirit has come within the love to assist and guide the one who is ready to depart.

If no spirits appear, I am the threshold guide. If the person in front of me is nonresponsive, I move my attention to my inner vision and meet her or him in the in-between worlds just beyond the physical. I hold no concept of what I may see nor hear, death is an individual experience.

This is where a soul may become trapped if there are fears or regrets. It is in this place that I speak to the person inwardly of those attachments or regrets. This is where I say, "Come this way!" showing the path, the light, and those who are waiting for the person on the other side.

There is little time involved in this process because consciousness is immediate, unlike words verbally spoken. My work is done when the departing Soul is smoothly drawn to those who await his arrival.

I do not transverse any symbol of passage with the person, tunnel, ocean, veil or simply and energetic shift. There is no need for me to do this because once the attachments to this world have been released and the other side is recognized, the person is drawn to it, like a moth to light. My job is done.

Chapter 9 – My Process

This work can be done remotely because time and space do not exist for consciousness. Consciousness is not limited to what the eyes see and the ears hear. It is who we are and all we have become as a vibrational awareness of incoming and outflowing information available to us. Consciousness is a unit of awareness open in proportion to what we have released in terms of attachments, specifically hooks that keep our attention locked within the physical world. It is my service to find the key and to unlock the hooks that cling to the mind and heart. SAFNAH is the bridge supporting the release of this life and the rebirth to the next.

My work and service continue from a residence I aptly call "The Lighthouse." My home on the Seacoast of New Hampshire is a solarium that was once a place where people were healed and moved on to new experiences in the physical or transitioned as souls back into the nonphysical. I am grateful to have this synchronistic reflection from the universe.

I asked a dear friend and Rabbinical student to help me find the word that expresses my work with the dying. He put two Hebraic roots together to form the word, *SAFNAH*, which translates into "death, birth, and threshold." I am *SAFNAH*, a person who is able to assist the dying over the threshold to the in-between worlds . . . where the light can be seen and where those loved ones wait to welcome the Soul home.

No matter the circumstance through these many decades of my life, or what work I have engaged in since a young child, I have been assisting souls through their final physical transformation. Always, within the Love.

Honoring Life's Process

Healing begins within one's own center. It is neither given nor applied. We learn how to honor our life's process as we grow within Spiritual understandings.

We learn to be within our own center, accepting with gratitude the varied opportunities life presents.

To fully live within our experiences, attaining enlightenment as a gift we give ourselves.

Life becomes an inner adventure, which reflects in our outer world as a harmonious dance with life.

Acknowledgments

It is with the deepest gratitude for the following people who offered their talents, support, and love in bringing this book and my life to fruition. For their friendship, dedication to humanity, and to all forms of life: Bru Brubaker who, while I was on Martha's Vineyard, first put a drum in my hand which immediately drew me to facilitate my first Soul Retrieval. I am forever indebted to you for unveiling my path.

Sofia Haffenreffer, DC, who posed the question, "What is the name of your work?" and William Haffenreffer, DC, who, with dedication and skill, has kept the Innate flowing through my spine as each threshold was crossed in the birthing of this book.

Nick Rudisill for taking the first very helpful look at the rough first draft.

Erika Hunter, author and editor, and friend for showing her love through editing and creating structure, and encouraging me in telling my story.

Llyn Roberts, teacher of Earth wisdom and award winning author, thank you for sharing the magic of this journey and for offering to be another set of eyes and heart, polishing the contents.

Audrey Jordan, artist extraordinaire, who painted "Visions of Heaven" and not only offered it for the book cover, but did all the graphics–you helped make this process fun.

Heidi Jordon for her skill with her camera and loving attention to every detail of producing the cover photograph.

Rabbi Jeff Amshalem for having the heart, taking time, and uncovering the two Hebraic roots that define my work as SAFNAH.

Gretchen Vogel, medium and author who, with open heart supported my process.

Sharon Lund of Sacred Life Publishers for her devotion to help support authors who have a message. She has made publishing a graceful experience. I also want to thank Sharon's team Miko Radcliffe and Mary Myers.

Those souls who honored me with their trust allowing me into their most sacred of times as they transitioned from this life into the next. Thank you for your teachings.

Lastly and, also firstly, Andrew Pashetto, who, when I was visiting in his Colorado home, brought out his Tarot deck and along with my son, Jacob White, gave me the kick I needed to finally write. They said, "What are you not doing that you must do?"

My response was, "Write my book."

Thank you to all my friends and family who have given me their loving support and encouragement, along with those mentioned, and who gave me strength and filled my heart. As always.

Acknowledgments

Thank you to my Nature guides and all guides in Spirit who have shown great patience with me as I have learned to listen and to do, who, with humor, sang hallelujah when I finally did hear.

About the Author

Rachel Leah

Rachel Leah has an associate degree from Boston University, is a Certified Nurses Assistant, ARC, a certification in Gerontology, and she has been initiated as a Reiki Master.

Rachel lives on the beautiful New Hampshire seacoast in an apartment she calls "The Lighthouse" once a hospital solarium where individuals healed or transitioned from the physical.

In Rachel's free time she enjoys being out in nature, watching her grandchildren grow, sharing time with friends and discovering new paradigms.

Rachel can be contacted through her web site: www.center-now.com or you can e-mail her at: journey@center-now.com.

Glossary

Astral Plane The vibrational level above the physical, attuned to the emotions, flying saucers, and ghosts.

Awareness The ability to observe and comprehend.

Causal Plane This is one of the mental planes where records of lives are kept and where one goes to learn the lessons of the previous life.

Center To draw the attention from the outside stimuli to within self.

Co-create The agreement to take action toward an outcome which is in accordance with the Divine Will. Some may call this action, perfect timing.

Consciousness The unit of awareness through which

	one perceives the person's reality.
Death	The release of the innate intelligence, consciousness, from physical form.
Etheric Plane	The fine vibration of the intuitions, just below soul plane.
He/She	In an attempt for universal cohesiveness I use he and she interchangeably.
Intuit	To be able to see and know without the use of physical means.
Life	The creative expression of consciousness.
Mental Plane	The place of thought and high-speed transmissions.
Reality	That which one knows to be true to itself.
SAFNAH	The combination of two Hebraic roots: death, birth threshold.
Self and self	The soul-connected Self and the ego-connected self.
Soul	An individual expression of

Glossary

accumulated wisdom, power, and love enveloped by a high vibrational field.

Soul Plane The home of consciousness, self-realization and 360-degree vision, the knowing.

Soul Retrieval The movement and transformation of a traumatized aspect of consciousness from a state of pain and loss to its original Soul's gift back to the consciousness from which it originated.

Spirit The divine spark of creativity.

Spirit Guide A spiritual helper in the nonphysical who communicates telepathically.

Surrender The releasing of all attachments, physically, emotionally, and mentally.

Transformation The movement from one state of reality to another.

Transition The movement of consciousness from one state of awareness to another.

Vibration The palpable manifestation of life.